KIDS RIVIERA
Sun & Fun Travel Focus

FIRST EDITION

Disclaimer

The information compiled in this book is for general information purposes only, with information based on my personal opinions/experiences from living on the French Riviera and additional information from cited sources. While all efforts have been made to include up-to-date and correct information, I make no representations or warranties of any kind, express or implied, about the completeness, accuracy, reliability, suitability or availability with respect to the information contained in this book for any purpose. Any reliance you place on such information is strictly at your own risk.

Defforge, Kim
KIDS RIVIERA — Sun & Fun Travel Focus
ISBN: 978-0-9888766-8-2

You can connect with the author at:

Blog: 24/7 in France
http://twentyfourseveninfrance.com
Email: twentyfourseveninfrance@gmail.com
Facebook: 24/7 in France
Twitter: 24_7France

Author of the following books (also available on Amazon):

♥ Solitary Desire – One Woman's Journey to France
♥ Sun, Sea & Savoir-Faire – Travel Focus on the French Riviera
♥ How To Write Your First Book – My Personal Step-by-Step Guide

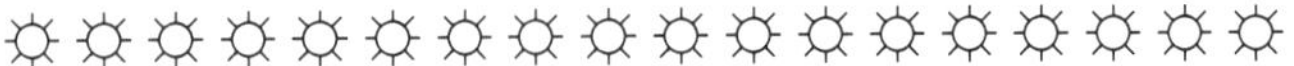

TABLE OF CONTENTS

KIDS RIVIERA

Sun & Fun Travel Focus

The French Riviera is full of sun & fun, with family-friendly activities for all ages. This travel focus is a compilation of easily accessible information, to help visitors discover and navigate the family side of the French Riviera. My hope is that you will take away wonderful memories of sun & fun from your stay – Bienvenue & Bon Séjour!

ANTIBES:

☺ **Espace Marineland**

Dolphins, sea lions, and sharks – Oh my – to get up close & personal! Shows, aquarium, penguins, shark tunnel, lemurs, polar bears, naval museum, and more!

http://www.marineland.fr/page-_en.php (English)
RN 7 – Route de Biot (National Route 7)
Tel: +33-(0)8-92-42-62-26 (0.34 cents/minute)
Open mid-February through September from 10 :00 a.m. – 7 :00 p.m (or until 11 :00 p.m., depending on the particular day)
Packages including other parks available or priced à la carte – see website for details.

☺ **Adventure Golf - Espace Marineland**

Mini-golf in a setting inspired by the novels of Jules Verne, with three 18-hole courses in the ambiance of the Lost World, with extraordinary landscapes of giant dinosaurs, waterfalls and fountains.

306 Av. Mozart
Tel: +33-(0)8-92-42-62-26
Open from 10:00 a.m. to 6:00 p.m. or 7:00 p.m. depending on the day; evening hours in July and August

☺ **Aquasplash at Espace Marineland**

The largest water park on the French Riviera - has pools and more than 2,000 meters of slides.

☺ **Antibes Land**

A large amusement park of over 30 attractions for children and adults.

Photo courtesy Nice Tourisme

RN 7 (across from Marineland) – Route de Biot
http://www.azurpark.com/anglais/antibes.html (English)
Tel : +33-(0)4-93-33-68-03
Weekends & holidays from 2 p.m. to 7 p.m.
Entry: Free

BAR-SUR-LOUP:

☺ Fun Kart

Located about 20 kms./1/2 hour from Nice, this is "the only outdoor track on the Riviera and one of the biggest in Europe." Go-kart rental (minimum age 7 years old) and other course options.
Open every day from 9:30 a.m. to 8:00 p.m. (schedules may change in winter).

Photo courtesy official brochure

Route de Gourdon
Le Bar-sur-Loup
Tel : +33-(0)4-93-42-48-08
www.fun-karting.com

BIOT :

☺ La Tasse de Couleur

A café for sweets, coffee, and tea; includes a studio where kids (and kids at heart) can paint their own ceramics and pottery. Prices include paints, brushes, sponges, etc, glazing and firing.

9, rue du Portugon in the center of the old village
Tel : 04-93-74-97-15
http://www.latassedecouleur.com/

Closed Sunday and Monday ; Wed. & Sat. 10 a.m.-6 p.m. and Tues. & Thurs. 2 – 6 p.m.
Open every day from 9:30 a.m. to 8:00 p.m., except closed on Monday and Tuesday from November to March (except holidays).

CAGNES-SUR-MER :

☺ Ecole Municipale de Voile (Sailing school)

Sailing and windsurfing lessons for ages 7 and up.

Photo: Nice Tourisme

http://www.cagnes-sur-mer.fr/ecole_voile/?page_id=449 (in French)

http://www.frenchriviera-tourism.com/seaside-resorts-beaches/ecole-de-voile-municipale-cagnes-sur-mer-N4fiche_ASCPAC0060000576-rub_2-act_VOILE,PLAVO.html
(in English)

CAILLE :

☺ **Arbre & Aventure**

Underground park adventure, chairlifts, all terrain biking, and much more.

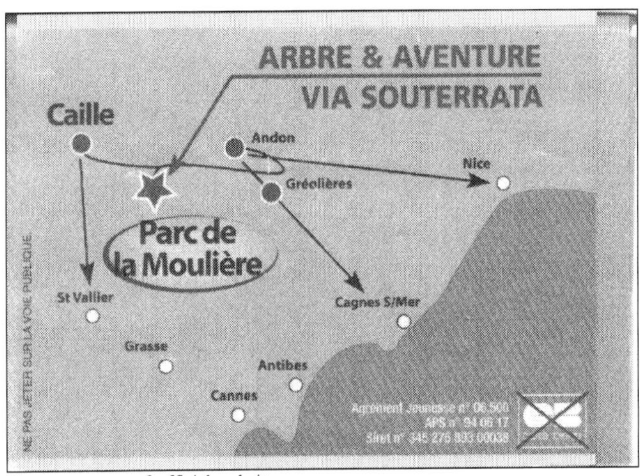

Photo courtesy of official website

Tel : +33-(0)4-93-36-60-57
Cell: +33-(0)6-60-52-66-25
www.arbreetaventure.fr
Email : cailleacrobranche@yahoo.fr
Open all year round

☺ VIA SOUTERRATA

Lou Païs
Tel : +33-(0)4-93-60-34-51
www.lou-pais.com
Email : loupais06@gmail.com

NOTE: Map indicates credit cards NOT accepted.

CANNES:

☺ Sainte-Marguerite Island / Lerins Islands

Discover the biological reserve of Ste.-Marguerite Island, where nature, culture, and relaxation away you. Home to Fort Royal and the Maritime Museum, where the cell that held the Man in the Iron Mask for 11 years can be seen.

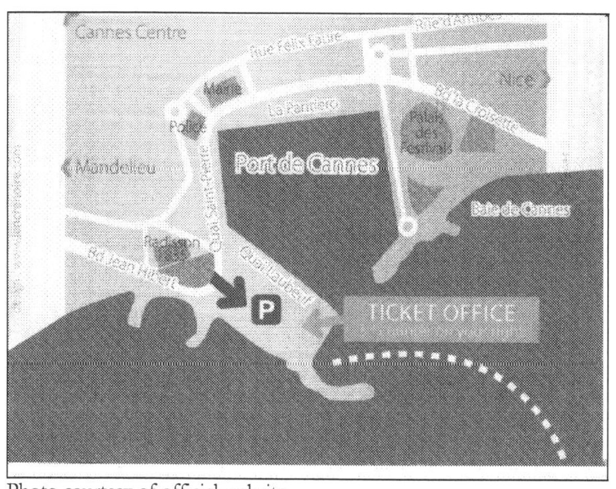

Photo courtesy of official website

The island is just a short boat ride from the Port in Cannes at Quai Laubeuf, with ongoing departures from 7:30 a.m., and runs every day including Sundays and public holidays. Ticket can be purchased on line: Adults: 12€ / Children (ages 5-10) 7.50€

http://www.trans-cote-azur.com/nice-ile-sainte-marguerite.php#
(ferry from Nice or Cannes)
Tel : +33-(0)4-92-98-71-30
Email : croisieres@trans-cote-azur.com

EZE:

☺ **Fragonard Perfumerie**
158 Avenue de Verdun
Tel: +33-(0)4 93 41 05 05

Situated between Nice and Monaco, accessible by bus #100 from Nice, this perfume, soap and cosmetics factory is a great site for the senses! They offer free guided tours, which ends with a visit to the luscious boutique.

Open every day, Sundays and public holidays included, from 8:30 a.m. to 6:30 p.m. (closed Noon to 2 p.m. from November to January).

JUAN-LES-PINS:

☺ Visiobulle

A glass-bottomed boat to get an underwater view of sea life. Boats depart from Ponton Courbet, running daily from April through September.

Photo courtesy Côte d'Azur Tourisme

www.visiobulle.com
Entry : 13€ (adults) & 6.50€ (ages 2-11)

MONACO:

☺ Jardin Exotique de Monaco (Exotic Garden)

Situated on a cliffside, with a panoramic view of Monaco, the exotic garden in Monaco features over a thousand species of cacti & succulents.

Open all year round (except Nov. 19 & Dec. 25) from 9 a.m.-5 p.m. (Jan/Nov/Dec) & from 9 a.m.-6 p.m. (Feb/March/April/Oct) and until 7 p.m. (May to Sept). Entrance ticket includes the visit to the garden, the Observatory Cave, and to the Anthropology Museum.

Photo courtesy of official brochure

62, Blvd du Jardin Exotique
Tel : +377-93-15-29-80
www.jardin-exotique.mc

☺ Musée Océanographique

Conceived as "a palace dedicated to the sea," the Oceanographic Museum features 6,500 m2 of marine life, over 6,000 specimens in their aquarium, recreated to their natural environment, a shark lagoon, and the "world's largest Curiosity Cabinet in a natural history museum."

Avenue St.-Martin
Tel: +377-93-15-36-00

Photo: Official brochure

☺ **Prince's Palace**
On the Palace Square (Place du Palais), the changing of the guards ceremony takes place daily at 11:55 a.m. sharp.

MOUGINS:

☺ **Boomiland**
A soft play area with slides, trampolines, climbing wall and a pool of plastic balls. There are two different areas for children of ages 1-3 and ages 3-12.
144 Chemin de la plaine
Tel: +33-(0)4-92-99-28-97
www.boomiland.fr

NICE:

☺ **Archeological Crypt**
An immense underground area of 2,000 m2 underneath Place Garibaldi.
Guided visits (one hour) daily, except Tuesday.

Place Jacques Toja
Tel: +33-(0)4-92-00-41-90
http://en.nicetourisme.com/things-to-do/27689 (English)
www.nice.fr/Culture/La-Crypte-Archeologique-de-Nice (French)
Entry: 5€ with reduced rates for seniors & students
Meeting point: Place Jacques Toja (near Place Garibaldi)

☺ Beaches

Jelly/plastic shoes are recommended to navigate the pebbly beaches. Not all beaches are lifeguard protected and also be alert for the (rare) presence of jellyfish: Medazur.fr and jellywatch.fr feature up-to-date sightings.

Life guarded beaches (with first aid stations) include Ponchette Plage, Beau Rivage, Lido Plage, Hi Beach, & Magnan; Ruhl Plage has a children's pool; water sports can be found at Opera & Blue Beach; sand volleyball court at Ponchette Plage; Neptune Beach has a children's playground.

☺ Colline du Château (Castle Hill)

At the East end of the Quai des Etats-Unis, this park and botanical garden is the site of the first town founded by the ancient Greeks, then the first medieval town, which today offers panoramic views over Nice and its surroundings, a surprising artificial waterfall, remains of the former 11th-century Cathedral, walkways paved with colorful 20th-century mosaics, a snack bar/café, a playground, and open spaces.

Photo credit: Nice Tourisme

Open daily 8 a.m. – 8 p.m. (summer) and 6 p.m. (winter) Entry: Free
Accessible by walking (92 m high), by elevator, and/or riding the Nice tourist train from the Promenade.

☺ **Fenocchio Ice Cream**
2, Place Rossetti in Old Nice
Open daily from 9 a.m. – Midnight (except from 10 a.m. on Monday)

Around 98 flavors of ice cream to suit everyone's sweet tooth!

☺ **Kid City**
An interior children's' play center – 700 square meters of slides, games, obstacle courses & more.

See video at http://www.kidscity.fr/

590, Route de Grenoble
Ground floor of Forum Lingostière (west of Nice)
Reservations Tel : +33-(0)4-92-01-10-70
Open 10-4 :30 p.m. or 10-7 p.m. depending on the week day
Entry : 6€ (under 4 years of age) & 10€ (ages 4-12)

☺ **Musée de la Curiosité**
Housing a restaurant, bar, & boutique, this is a site featuring children's theater & magic shows (in French) in its various rooms.
39, rue Beaumont near the Nice Port/Republique area
Tel: +33-(0)4-92-04-69-32
www.museedelacuriosite.com
Video: http://youtu.be/mnthC6r3-0s.

Open every day from 2 – 7 p.m. (except during school vacation breaks)
Guided visits held every hour.
Entry: 8€ per person (all ages)

☺ Observatoire de Nice
www.obs-nice.fr
Info: +33-(0)4-93-85-85-58 or (0)4-92-00-31-12
Wed. & Sat. at 2:45 p.m.
Park hours: Wed. at 9:45 a.m. & Sat. at 2:15 p.m.

Only 4.5 km from Nice on the Grande Corniche by car or bus #84 from Nice-Riquier train station, the Observatory is situated in a forest of about 77 acres of rare and protected vegetation. Guided walks available.

☺ Parc Regional du Mercantour
About 70 km from Nice, this national park in the Alpes-Maritimes has around 600 km of marked footpaths and comprises 7 valleys, 28 villages, and 150 rural sites.

(nearby) Park Alpha – Wolf Park
Chalet d'Accueil du Boréon – Saint-Martin Vesubie
The wolf park welcomes you all year long from 10 a.m. to 5 or 6 p.m. (see schedule on website)
http://www.alpha-loup.com/anglais/accueil.php
Tel: +33 (0)4-93-02-33-69
The Park is situated at a 1500 meter altitude, so dress accordingly. The visit lasts 2-½ hours minimum.

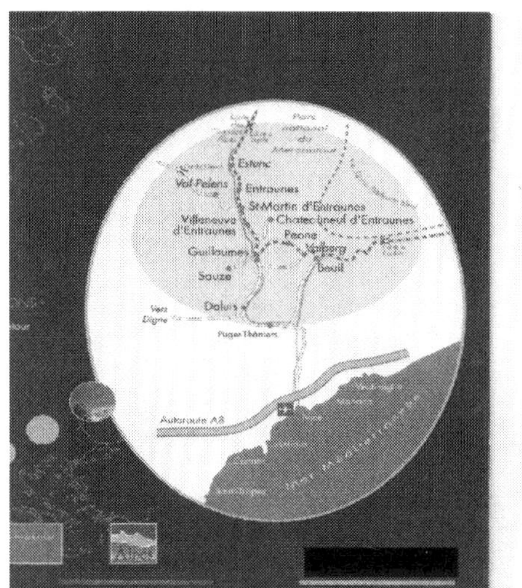

Photo source: Office de Tourisme Les Portes du Mercantour

☺ Parc Phoenix

www.parc-phoenix.org

This 15-acre/7 hectare park is ideally located (near the Nice Airport) and is an affordable family place to take in the park's open spaces, a variety of gardens, aquarium, and a butterfly pavillion.

Photo: Nice Tourisme

Entry 2€ - free entry for children under 12

☺ Park Thorenc

The Domaine de Haut Thorenc is where bison and wild horses, deer, and wild boar roam free and can be seen from the tour-guided, horse driven carriages (calèches). Situated at over 1,000 meters in altitude, it can be cool even in summer; within walking distance to the Crètes du Domaine and the ruins of the Château Templier du Castellaras.

☺ Promenade des Anglais

Nice's 7 km. (4.2 miles) seafront walkway, just perfect for strolling, cycling, biking, and rollerblading. Take in the view of the Mediterranean, while sitting on one of the Prom's iconic blue chairs, or relax at one of the seaside restaurants closer to the water's edge.

VéloBlue is the city's bike rental program, with about 175 automated locations. You must register by phone and provide a credit card - first ½ hour use free.

Photo: Nice Tourisme

Roller Station
49, quai des Etats-Unis
Tel : +33-(0)8-99-02-16-72 (not a free call)
Open everyday and all year long.
Rental Fees:
Bikes: 5€ per hour & 7€ for two hours
Roller: 5€ per hour & 6 € for two hours

☺ Promenade du Paillon

A new, 12-hectare/26 acres pedestrian green-zone park is host to playgrounds with wooden animal creatures (whale, dolphin, turtle, octopus) and lots of open space, winding from the Jardin Albert I up to the Théatre de Nice.

Photos credit: 24/7 in France

☺ Tourist Train

A 45-minute circuit through Old Town, Place Garibaldi & the Port area, and up to Castle Hill, where it stops for 10 minutes; running commentary headsets. Departures every 30 minutes on the seafront Promenade, opposite the Albert 1st gardens.

Tel: +33 (0)2-99-88-47-07
www.ttdf.com
Price: 8€ /children under 12 at 4€

☺ Train de Digne (Steam engine train from Nice to Puget-Théniers & Annot)

Leaving from the train station Chemin de Fer de Provence (near Malaussena in the Liberation neighborhood), this charming train runs through the Mediterranean back country, with stops in Entrevaux (for photos only) and longer stops in Annot and Puget-Théniers for a picturesque day's outing.

Tel: +33-(0)4-97-03-80-80
www.trainprovence.com
http://www.trainprovence.com/pages/fr/236/plan-de-la-ligne.html
Roundtrip: (aller-retour): 37€ (age 4-12 is 27€)

☺ Hiking/Biking/Skiing

About 1 ½ - 2 hours from Nice, the ski/summer resorts of Auron and Isola 2000 are a perfect place to hike, mountain bike, or ski – depending on the season. Bus transportation from Nice takes about 2 hours.

Tel (Auron) : +33-(0)4-93-23-02-66
www.auron.com

Isola 2000 : http://hiver.isola2000.com
http://ete.isola2000.com

Neige (snow) bus information : www.cg06.fr

ST-JEAN-CAP-FERRAT :

☺ **Musée des Coquillages**

This seashell museum holds diverse collections of species found in the Mediterranean Sea and includes a 7-minute panoramic presentation and optional guided visit.

Quai du Vieux Port
Tel : +33-(0)4-93-76-17-61
www.musee-coquillages.com

Open Monday through Friday from 10 a.m. – Noon & 2 p.m. to 6 p.m.
Weekends and holidays from 2 p.m. to 6 p.m.
Adults: 2€ entry
Under 15 years of age, students, & handicapped: 1€ entry
Group of 10 or more: 1.50€ per person

☺ Sentier du Littoral

Pedestrian coastal walks, varying in terrain and length, allow you to explore the rugged coastline. Check with the local tourist offices for a map and detailed information.

The most well known are:

- Le Cap Ferrat around the peninsula of Saint-Jean Cap Ferrat
- Le Cap d'Antibes
- le Cap de Nice to Villefranche
- Le Cap d'Ail to Monaco

ST LAURENT-DU-VAR:

☺ Centre Nautique

Nautical center, located just west of Nice, offering kayaking, wind-surfing, kite-surfing, water skiing, and sailing by the week, hour, or half-day. English spoken.

Photo courtesy Bateaux

416, avenue Donadeï
Tél. +33-(0)4-93-07-53-73
c.nautique@agasc.fr

Activities listing:
http://www.cotedazur-tourisme.com/mer-plages/centre-nautique-de-saint-laurent-du-var-st-laurent-du-var-N4fiche_ASCPAC0060000024-rub_2.html

VILLEFRANCHE :

☺ **Excursions Acti Loisirs**
A 100-passenger boat will take you out 20 nautical miles from the coast to look at dolphins and whales. A naturalist guide will tell you about the sea life you will meet during the trip.

Gare Maritime du Port de la Santé
Tel. : +33-(0)-6-01-33-42-68
http://www.dauphin-mediterranee.com

VILLENEUVE-LOUBET :

☺ **Canyon Forest**
There are four courses (varying by level of difficulty) throughout this adventure park with zip lines, rope bridges, and oversized swings, canyoning, and rock climbing.

1, Avenue de la Liberation
Reservations required : Tel. +33-(0)4-92-02-88-88

www.canyonforest.com
See video on website home page

Open weekends, holidays, and Wednesday afternoons beginning April; Open every day in July and August
25€ adults and 22€ children (8-17 years old) / group pricing for 5 or more / under 16 years old must be accompanied by an adult

☺ Le Bois des Lutins

For kids from age 2 to 102, this 4-hectare (8.8 acres) nature park has a multitude of fun activities for the whole family: netted tree climbing, bridges, and slides, intertube slides, zip lines (near ground level), playgrounds, & much more ! Situated between Nice and Grasse, off Autoroute A8 - Exit 47.

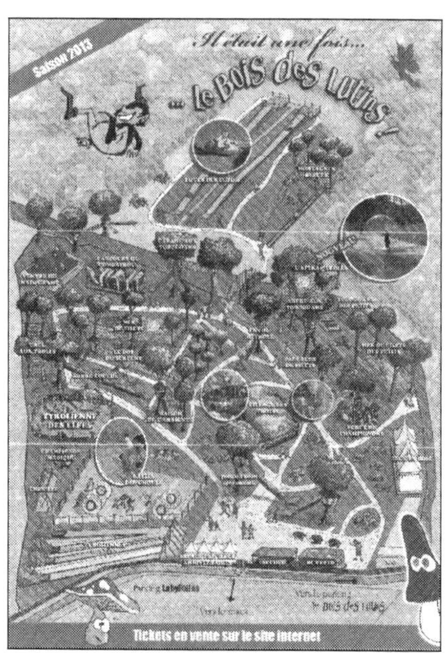

Photo: Official brochure

Tel : +33-(0)4-92-02-06-06
www.leboisdeslutins.com (see video on home page)
Email : azurlabyrinthe@wanadoo.fr
Entry: 14.50€ (ages 2-4 at 7.50€)
Must show ID to enter

☺ **Le Pitchoun Forest (nearby to Canyon Forest)**
A park of four climbing courses of games and challenges, with varying themes.

http://www.azur-labyrinthe.com/anglais/angindex2.html (in English)
See video on website home page
Entry : 15€ per child

MISC:

☺ **Nice Airport information for Unaccompanied Minors Traveling Alone**
http://en.nice.aeroport.fr/Passengers/PASSENGER-INFO/Need-help/Unaccompanied-Minors-UM

☺ **Kids & Teens Summer Camp & French Courses (site in English)**
http://www.cia-france.com/kids-teens/nice-activities.php

☺ **Youth Information Offices (*Bureaux Information Jeunesse* - BIJ)**
The following offices can provide information on activities and associations for children throughout the Alpes-Maritimes region.

Nice Notre-Dame Info Jeunesse
21 rue d'Angleterre / Tel: +33-(0)4-93-82-40-42

Antibes Info Jeunesse
18-20 boulevard Foch / Tel: +33-(0)4-92-90-52-38

Cannes Info Jeunesse
5 quai Saint Pierre / Tel: +33-(0)4-97-06-46-25

Grasse Info Jeunesse
16 chemin de Camperousse
Le Plan de Grasse
Tel: +33-(0)4-97-05-00-00

Menton Info Jeunesse
Place Ardoïno / Tel: +33-(0)4-93-28-60-50

☺ **Summer Camp for Kids & Teens (site in French)**
http://www.lescolos.com

☺ **Information Jeunesse Côte d'Azur (site in French)**
http://www.ijca.fr/

Merci for reading Kids Riviera - Sun & Fun Travel Focus!

Author's Bio:

Born in the U.S., and now living on the French Riviera, Kim enjoys the savoir-faire of French culture and all that the region has to offer. As a former French teacher, lifelong Francophile, and having worked in Nice, she currently write books and share news, information, & amusing stories on the blog "24/7 in France."

You can connect with the author at:

Blog: 24/7 in France
http://twentyfourseveninfrance.com
Email: twentyfourseveninfrance@gmail.com
Facebook: 24/7 in France
Twitter: 24_7France

Author of the following books:
(also available on Amazon)

♥ Solitary Desire – One Woman's Journey to France
♥ Sun, Sea & Savoir-Faire – Travel Focus on the French Riviera
♥ How To Write Your First Book – My Personal Step-by-Step Guide

Made in the USA
Middletown, DE
03 February 2022